Jacine Star

THE INCOME CATALYST

Unleashing the Power of Multiple Streams of Income

Contents

Introduction

Hello and welcome to "The Income Catalyst: Unleashing the Power of Multiple Streams of Income." Traditional concepts of income production are being challenged in today's rapidly changing world. The age-old paradigm of relying on a single job or source of income to achieve financial stability and prosperity is no longer sufficient. It's time to adopt a new mindset—one that allows you to tap into the tremendous possibilities of many revenue streams.

This book will walk you through the process of unlocking the possibilities and opportunities that exist in the field of earning various streams of income. Whether you're an aspiring entrepreneur, a seasoned professional, or someone looking for financial freedom, this book will provide you with the knowledge, methods, and inspiration required to go on a financial abundance path.

We'll go over practical procedures and tried-and-true techniques for identifying and cultivating multiple revenue streams that correspond with your abilities, passions, and market needs, chapter by chapter. You will learn how to traverse the terrain of revenue production like never before, from using your knowledge in a digital environment to embracing the power of automation and delegation.

But this book is about more than just making money; it's about living a life of freedom, flexibility, and fulfillment. It's about discovering your route to financial security while pursuing your passions and living a lifestyle that reflects your values.

Are you ready to realize your true earning potential? Are you ready to take the plunge, free from the constraints of a single source of income, and embrace a life of abundance? If so, let "The Income Catalyst" be your guide as we embark on this life-changing journey together. Prepare to unleash the potential of many revenue streams and pave the way to a more successful future.

Chapter 1

Identifying potential streams of income

1.   Assessing your skills and passion

Assessing your skills and passions is a must when it comes to generating multiple streams of income. By understanding your unique abilities and interests, you can find income opportunities that not only match your skills but also bring you joy and fulfillment.

Here are some key points to consider when assessing your skills and passions:

Take some time to reflect on your strengths: Consider both hard skills (technical abilities, specialized knowledge) and soft skills (communication, problem-solving, leadership). Think about tasks or activities that come naturally to you and where you excel. These strengths will serve as a solid foundation for developing income streams that leverage your expertise.

Look for transferable skills: Don't limit yourself to a narrow view. Look for transferable skills that can be applied across different industries or income streams. For example, if you have excellent project management skills, you can apply them in various contexts, such as freelancing, consulting, or starting a business.

Explore your passions: Passion plays a significant role in finding income streams that bring you long-term satisfaction. Think about the activities or topics that ignite your enthusiasm and curiosity. Consider your hobbies, interests, and causes that you deeply care about. When you're passionate about what you do, you're more likely to stay motivated and dedicated, even when faced with challenges.

Seek feedback and external perspectives: It can be challenging to objectively assess our skills and passions. Reach out to trusted friends, colleagues, or mentors who can provide valuable insights about your strengths and areas where they believe you excel. Their perspectives can shed light on aspects you might not have considered or recognized in yourself.

Embrace continuous learning: Assessing your skills and passions should be an ongoing process. The world is constantly evolving, and new opportunities emerge regularly. Stay curious and commit to lifelong learning. Invest in personal development, attend workshops or courses, and explore emerging trends in your areas of interest. By expanding your skill set, you open doors to new income streams that may not have been available to you before.

Remember, assessing your skills and passions is about self-awareness and introspection. It's an opportunity to understand your unique value proposition and uncover the areas where you can make a meaningful impact. By leveraging your strengths and pursuing your passions, you'll be on your way to creating multiple streams of income that align with who you are and what you love to do.

2. Research Market Demand

Researching market demand is also essential when it comes to identifying viable income streams. Understanding the needs, preferences, and trends of your target audience allows you to align your skills and passions with income-generating opportunities that have a higher chance of success.

Here are some key considerations when researching market demand:

Clearly define your target audience: Understand their characteristics, demographics, behaviors, and pain points. This will help you tailor your income streams to their needs and preferences effectively. Conduct market research: Use a variety of research methods to gather information about your target audience and the market landscape. This can include surveys, interviews, focus groups, online forums, social media listening, and competitor analysis.

Identify gaps and opportunities: Analyze the data collected during your market research to identify gaps or underserved areas in the market. Look for unmet needs, pain points, or areas where existing solutions are lacking. These gaps represent potential opportunities for you to create income streams that address those specific needs or offer a unique value proposition.

Stay abreast of industry trends: follow industry publications, attend conferences or webinars, and engage with relevant online communities. By staying informed, you can anticipate emerging needs and adapt your income streams accordingly, ensuring their relevance and longevity.

Test and validate your ideas: Once you have identified potential income streams based on your skills and market research, it's essential to validate their viability. Try out your ideas on a small scale, get feedback from your intended audience, and make changes based on their reactions. This iterative approach helps you to perfect your offerings and make sure they meet the needs of the market.

Continually Monitor and Adjust: Market needs are ever-changing, so it's essential to keep an eye on them and make changes to your income streams as needed. Pay attention to customer feedback, industry trends, and changes in the competitive landscape. Be willing to make modifications to your offerings to stay up-to-date and meet the current market demands. It's important to remember that researching market demand is an ongoing process. It requires a combination of data analysis, customer insights, and industry knowledge. By understanding your target audience and the market environment, you can create multiple income streams that are not only in demand but also have the potential for long-term success.

3. Brainstorming Income Ideas

Generating multiple streams of income is an exciting and creative process that allows you to explore various opportunities.

Here are some steps to help you effectively brainstorm income ideas:

Assess Your Skills and Passions: Start by assessing your skills and passions. Identify the areas where you excel and have a genuine interest. Consider how you can use these skills and passions to create income-generating opportunities.

Research Different Business Models: Familiarize yourself with various business models that align with your skills and interests. For example, you could explore freelancing, consulting, e-commerce, content creation, rental properties, investments, or affiliate marketing. Each model has its advantages and requirements, so explore which ones resonate with you and offer the potential for multiple income streams.

Identify Problems and Solutions: Think about common issues or challenges that people or businesses face. Brainstorm ideas for how you can provide solutions to these problems through your skills or expertise. Consider both traditional and innovative approaches to address these issues.

Combine and Cross-Pollinate Ideas: Look for ways to combine different skills or passions to create unique income streams. For example, if you have a knack for photography and love traveling, you could create a travel photography blog, offer photography services to travel companies, or sell prints of your travel photos online. Cross-pollinating ideas allow you to tap into multiple interests and increase your income potential.

Study Successful Case Studies: Study successful entrepreneurs or individuals who have generated multiple streams of income. Research their business models, strategies, and income streams. While you should never copy someone else's idea directly, these case studies can provide inspiration and insights into what works in different industries.

Explore Online Opportunities: In today's digital age, there are numerous online opportunities to explore. Think about how you can use the internet to reach a wider audience, offer digital products or services, or create online communities. The online realm provides a vast landscape for generating income streams, so explore the possibilities it offers. Evaluate

Feasibility and Scalability: As you brainstorm ideas, consider the feasibility and scalability of each income stream. Assess factors such as the initial investment required, time commitment, market demand, competition, and growth potential. Prioritize ideas that are both realistic and have the potential for scalability in the long run.

Iterate and Refine: Brainstorming is an iterative process. Don't be afraid to generate multiple ideas, even if some initially seem far-fetched. Review and refine your list of ideas, eliminating those that are not viable or don't align with your goals. Narrow down your options to a few ideas that have the most potential and resonate with you the most.

Remember, brainstorming income ideas is about exploring possibilities and thinking outside the box. It's a creative process that allows you to combine your skills, passions, and market demand to generate multiple streams of income that are unique to you. Be open to experimentation and adapt your ideas as you gain insights and feedback along the way.

Chapter 2

Developing multiple streams of Income

Welcome to Chapter 2 of "The Income Catalyst: Unleashing the Power of Multiple Streams of Income." Now that you have identified potential income sources based on your skills, passions, and market demand, it's time to explore the process of developing and nurturing these streams into sustainable sources of revenue.

In this chapter, we will discuss key strategies and principles that will guide you on your journey toward creating multiple streams of income. Developing multiple streams of income is not just about diversifying your sources of revenue; it's about building a resilient and adaptable income portfolio that supports your financial goals and aspirations. By having multiple income streams, you create a more secure and stable foundation that can withstand economic uncertainties, industry changes, and personal circumstances. In this chapter, we will address the following critical aspects of developing multiple streams of income: Prioritize and Focus: To effectively develop multiple income streams, it's important to prioritize and focus on a few key opportunities initially. By concentrating your efforts and resources on a select few, you can dedicate the necessary time and attention to develop them to their full potential.

This focused approach allows you to lay a solid foundation before expanding into additional income streams. Build Your Brand: Your brand is an essential asset when it comes to generating multiple streams of income. We will discuss the importance of establishing a strong online presence, creating a professional portfolio, and cultivating a reputation for excellence in your chosen areas. A well-crafted personal brand helps you attract clients, customers, and opportunities that align with your expertise and values.

Diversify Your Income Streams: Building multiple streams of income requires diversification. We will explore the concept of diversifying your income streams by offering different products or services, exploring various industries or niches, or investing in different asset classes. Diversification not only mitigates the risk of relying on a single source of income but also opens up opportunities for growth and stability. Throughout this chapter, we will provide useful insights, tips, and actionable steps to help you navigate the development of multiple streams of income. You will learn how to optimize your time and resources, leverage your skills and passions, and adapt to changing market dynamics. By the end of this chapter, you will have a solid understanding of how to build and nurture a diverse income portfolio that supports your financial aspirations. Are you ready to take the next step toward creating multiple streams of income? Let's dive into Chapter 2 and explore the strategies that will empower you to develop your income streams and unlock your full earning potential.

1. Prioritizing and Focus

Prioritizing and focusing is essential when it comes to creating multiple sources of income. It's important to concentrate your efforts and resources on a few key opportunities to ensure their successful development.

Here's a closer look at how to prioritize and focus on your income streams:

Evaluate Potential Income Streams: Examine the potential income streams you identified during the assessment phase. Consider factors such as market demand, profitability, scalability, and personal interest. Rank the opportunities based on their potential to generate income and align with your long-term goals.

Set Clear Goals: Establish clear objectives for each income stream you prioritize. These goals should be specific, measurable, achievable, relevant, and time-bound (SMART). Define what success looks like for each stream and determine the milestones or targets you want to reach. Having clear goals provides direction and helps you stay focused on the most important income opportunities.

Allocate Time and Resources: Once you have identified your priority income streams and set goals, allocate your time and resources accordingly. Decide how much time you can dedicate to each stream and allocate resources such as finances, tools, and support accordingly. By allocating resources strategically, you ensure that each income stream receives the necessary attention and investment for growth.

Develop Action Plans: Create action plans for each priority income stream. Break down the steps required to develop and monetize each stream, considering aspects such as product or service development, marketing and promotion, client acquisition, and revenue generation. Set deadlines and milestones within your action plans to keep yourself accountable and track progress.

Implement and Iterate: Start taking action on your plans and implement your strategies for each income stream. Monitor the results and gather feedback along the way. Be open to making adjustments and iterations based on the insights you gain and the market response. Stay focused on the priorities while remaining flexible to optimize your income streams' performance.

Assess and Reassess: Regularly evaluate the performance and potential of your income streams. Assess if they are meeting your goals, if there are any emerging opportunities or challenges, and if adjustments need to be made. As you gain more experience and insights, you may need to reassess your priorities and make necessary shifts to optimize your income portfolio.

Gradually Expand: Once your priority income streams are well-established and generating stable income, you can consider expanding into additional streams. Growing your income portfolio should be a gradual process that allows you to maintain focus and ensure the sustainability of each stream. By expanding strategically, you can diversify your sources of revenue further and enhance your overall financial stability. Remember, prioritizing and focusing are key to effectively developing multiple streams of income. By concentrating your efforts on a select few opportunities and diligently working towards their success, you increase your chances of building sustainable and lucrative income streams. Stay committed to your priorities, be open to change, and monitor progress to achieve your income goals.

2. Developing your Brand

Developing your brand is an essential part of creating multiple sources of income. A powerful personal brand can help you stand out from the crowd, gain credibility, draw in opportunities, and connect with your target audience.

Here are some key steps to consider when constructing your brand:

Define Your Brand Identity: Begin by defining your brand identity—what you want to be known for, your values, and your unique selling point. Clarify your mission, vision, and the value you bring to the table. Identify your strengths, expertise, and the qualities that make you different from others in your field. This self-awareness forms the basis of your brand.

Construct Your Brand Story: Your brand story is the narrative that communicates who you are, your journey, and why you do what you do. Create an engaging and genuine story that resonates with your target audience. Share your experiences, challenges, and successes in a way that connects with others on an emotional level. Your brand story should demonstrate your expertise, enthusiasm, and the value you offer.

Develop a Professional Online Presence: Establishing a strong online presence is essential in today's digital world. Start by creating a professional website that displays your brand, highlights your expertise, and provides a platform for your content. Optimize your social media profiles to reflect your brand identity consistently. Engage with your audience on social media platforms by sharing valuable content, interacting with others in your field, and participating in relevant conversations.

Share Valuable Content: Position yourself as a thought leader and expert by consistently sharing valuable content related to your areas of expertise. Create blog posts, videos, podcasts, or social media content that educates, informs, and motivates your audience. Customize your content to address their pain points, answer their questions, and provide practical solutions. Regularly publishing high-quality content helps you build credibility, attract an audience, and establish yourself as an authority in your field.

Foster Relationships and Networks: Actively engage with your audience, industry peers, and influencers in your field.

Attend conferences, webinars, and networking events to connect with like-minded individuals and potential collaborators or clients. Build genuine relationships by offering value, being supportive, and participating in relevant discussions. Cultivating relationships helps expand your network, opens doors to collaboration opportunities, and increases your brand visibility.

Seek Testimonials and Social Proof: Encourage satisfied clients, customers, or colleagues to provide testimonials or reviews that highlight the value you've delivered. Display these testimonials on your website or social media profiles to establish social proof and build trust with potential clients or customers. Positive feedback from others strengthens your brand reputation and boosts your credibility.

Continuously Learn and Improve: Invest in continuous learning and professional development to stay relevant and enhance your expertise. Attend workshops, conferences, or courses to expand your knowledge and skills. Stay up to date on industry trends, emerging technologies, and best practices. Demonstrating a commitment to learning and improvement reinforces your brand as someone who stays ahead of the curve.

Constructing your brand is an ongoing process that requires consistency, authenticity, and dedication. Stay true to your brand values and continuously refine your message and offerings as you gain experience and feedback. A strong personal brand will attract opportunities, elevate your visibility, and contribute to the success of your multiple income streams.

The Importance of Brand Development

Creating your brand is essential for various reasons:

Differentiation: In a congested marketplace, a strong brand can help you stand out. It enables you to distinguish yourself by emphasizing your unique value proposition, personality, and distinguishing characteristics. A well-developed brand explains to potential customers and clients why they should choose you over others who offer comparable products or services.

Trust and Credibility: A powerful brand instills trust and credibility in your target audience. People are more inclined to choose your products or services when they recognize and trust your brand. You develop a positive reputation that fosters trust and loyalty by regularly delivering on your brand promises and maintaining high standards.

Customer Loyalty: A well-developed brand fosters customer loyalty. Customers are more likely to become repeat customers and advocates if they have a pleasant experience with your brand and feel a connection to it. Repeat business and word-of-mouth referrals are important growth and profitability drivers.

Emotional Connection: Brands have the potential to connect emotionally with their target audience. When your brand elicits good emotions and resonates with the values, ambitions, or aspirations of your target market, it promotes a deeper relationship. Long-term client relationships and enhanced customer lifetime value can result from emotional ties.

Price Premium: With a strong brand, you may command a higher price for your products or services. Customers are typically prepared to pay more for your brand if they perceive it to be high-quality, dependable, and unique. A well-known brand can assist you in positioning yourself as a premium offering in the market, enhancing profitability and revenue potential.

Attracting Talented Employees and Potential Partners: A great brand draws both talented employees and potential partners. A great brand story and reputation may make your company an enticing place to work, attracting top individuals who share your values. Furthermore, powerful brands are more likely to attract strategic alliances and collaborations, which will broaden your reach and chances.

Expansion and Diversification: A well-developed brand serves as a solid platform for future growth and diversification. It becomes easier to introduce additional items or services under the same brand umbrella if your brand has established reputation and loyalty. Based on this, your existing customer base is more likely to test your new services.

Crisis Resilience: Having a strong brand allows you to more effectively manage and recover from crises. Customers are more inclined to support you during difficult times if you have a well-established brand and good ties with them. Negative occurrences or situations can be mitigated by a positive brand reputation and trustworthiness.

Long-Term Business Value: A strong brand is valuable in the long run. Brands can be important assets that add to the total value of a company. When you create a recognizable and trustworthy brand, it can become an intangible asset that increases the desirability of your company to potential investors, buyers, or partners.

Consistency and Focus: Developing your brand necessitates defining your fundamental beliefs and target audience and distinct location. This activity helps you keep your messaging, marketing initiatives, and business decisions focused and consistent. A well-defined brand strategy acts as a guiding foundation for all parts of your organization, ensuring a unified and coherent approach.

Brand development is critical for differentiation, trust, customer loyalty, emotional connection, pricing premium, attracting talent and partners, expansion, crisis resilience, long-term economic value, and sustaining consistency and focus. Investing in the development and maintenance of your brand can result in large profits and long-term competitive advantage.

3. Diversifying your income streams

Diversifying your income sources is a key strategy for reducing risk, increasing stability, and maximizing your earning potential. Relying on a single source of income leaves you exposed to changes in the market or unexpected circumstances. By diversifying, you can create a more resilient income portfolio.

Here is a closer look at how to diversify your income streams:

Identify Different Income Streams: Begin by identifying various income streams that are compatible with your skills, passions, and market demand. Consider the different business models and opportunities available, such as freelancing, consulting, passive income, investments, royalties, or creating and selling products or services. Brainstorm ideas and explore opportunities in both traditional and emerging industries.

Leverage Your Existing Expertise: Look for ways to leverage your existing expertise or skills to create additional income streams. Identify areas where your knowledge and experience can be applied in different ways. For example, if you have expertise in graphic design, you could offer design services, create and sell digital products, teach design courses, or start a design consultancy. Leveraging your expertise allows you to capitalize on what you already know while branching out into different avenues.

Explore Different Industries or Niches: Consider broadening your income streams by exploring different industries or niches. Look for opportunities where your skills or knowledge can be applied in new and untapped markets. For instance, if you're a fitness enthusiast, you could consider offering online fitness coaching, writing fitness-related books or articles, creating fitness-related digital products, or starting a fitness-focused YouTube channel. Exploring new industries or niches allows you to tap into different target audiences and revenue sources.

Create Passive Income Streams: Passive income streams are those that generate revenue with minimal ongoing effort or time investment. They can provide a steady income source while allowing you to focus on other income-generating activities. Explore opportunities such as rental properties, affiliate marketing, online courses, e-books, royalties from intellectual property, or investments in stocks, bonds, or real estate. Passive income streams can provide long-term financial stability and free up time for pursuing other ventures.

Develop Multiple Products or Services: Within each income stream, consider diversifying further by developing multiple products or services. This allows you to cater to a wider range of customer needs and preferences. For example, if you offer consulting services, you could create different service packages, online courses, or informational products to reach a broader audience. Developing multiple offerings within each income stream increases your revenue potential and appeals to a diverse customer base.

Evaluate and Monitor Performance: Regularly evaluate the performance of each income stream to determine its profitability, growth potential, and alignment with your goals. Assess the time and resources invested versus the return generated. Identify any income streams that are underperforming or no longer viable, and consider reallocating those resources to more promising opportunities. Ongoing evaluation ensures that your income streams remain effective and aligned with your overall strategy.

Adapt to Market Trends and Opportunities: Stay aware of market trends, customer needs, and emerging opportunities. Be open to adapting your income streams to meet changing demands or capitalize on new market developments. This could involve exploring emerging technologies, adjusting pricing or packaging, expanding into complementary areas, or collaborating with other professionals or businesses. By adapting and staying flexible, you can seize opportunities and stay ahead in the market.

Diversifying your income streams requires careful planning, ongoing evaluation, and a willingness to explore new possibilities. It allows you to mitigate risk, maximize your earning potential, and create a more stable and sustainable income portfolio. Continuously assess and refine your income streams to ensure they remain relevant, profitable, and aligned with your long-term goals.

The Importance of Income Stream Diversification

Diversifying revenue sources is important for various reasons:

Danger Reduction: Relying on a single source of income puts you in greater danger. Economic downturns, disruptions in the sector, or personal situations can all have a detrimental impact on that income stream. Diversifying your income across numerous sources reduces risk and provides a safety net if one stream fails. If one source of income is disrupted, the others can continue to give financial security.

Increased Financial Stability and Resilience: Having various revenue streams provides a more robust financial basis. If one stream has fluctuations or seasonal variances, others can make up the difference. This steadiness allows you to easily withstand unforeseen bills, economic concerns, or personal difficulties.

Increased Financial Security: Diversification minimizes risk and reduces your reliance on a single income or client, resulting in more financial security. It provides you with a buffer to deal with unanticipated occurrences or financial setbacks. Having various income streams lessens the risk of relying entirely on one source and provides security and peace of mind.

Revenue Growth and Wealth Creation: By diversifying your revenue streams, you can increase your chances of growth and wealth creation. Each revenue source has growth potential, and by combining them, you may boost your entire earning potential. Different sources of income may increase at different rates, and by taking advantage of diverse chances, you can accelerate your financial progress and attain your goals more quickly.

Increasing Knowledge and Skill Sets: Managing various streams of income frequently necessitates the acquisition of new abilities and information. You may study other industries, pursue entrepreneurial initiatives, or make investments as you diversify. This diversification broadens your knowledge base, broadens your skill sets, and exposes you to new experiences and viewpoints. It can lead to personal development and the acquisition of transferable skills.

Entrepreneurial Opportunities: Diversifying income streams frequently involves entrepreneurial efforts such as launching a side business, freelancing, or investing in initiatives. These business alternatives not only create revenue, but also allow for creativity, autonomy, and personal fulfillment. They have the potential to become lucrative assets that increase in value over time.

Flexibility and Freedom: Having many revenue streams allows you to manage your time and resources more effectively. You have greater influence over your financial fate because you are not employed exclusively dependent on a single employer or client. Diversification can help you achieve a work-life balance that matches your priorities and allows you to pursue passions or personal interests in addition to earning a living.

Passive Income: The ability to earn passive income is provided through diversifying income streams. Passive income streams, such as rental properties, investments, royalties, or online enterprises, can create income without requiring continuous active labor. Over time, these passive income streams can give financial stability, boost cash flow, and develop wealth.

Market Adaptation: Diversification makes you more adaptive to shifting market conditions and trends. Consumer preferences change as industries evolve. You can adapt to these changes more easily if you have various revenue streams. If one income stream becomes outmoded or less profitable, you can reallocate resources to another that is more in line with current market demands.

Overall Financial Freedom: Diversifying revenue streams is the first step toward financial freedom. You have greater control over your financial destiny by lowering your reliance on a single income or company. It enables you to make decisions based on your objectives, desires, and values rather than financial constraints. Financial independence gives you the flexibility to pursue your passions.

Diversifying income streams provides risk reduction, stability, resilience, financial security, income growth, skill development, entrepreneurial opportunities, flexibility, passive income, adaptation, and a route to financial independence. You build a strong financial structure that supports your goals by diversifying your revenue.

Stages of Wealth Creation

Individual circumstances, techniques, and aspirations can all influence the stages of wealth generation. However, the following is a broad framework outlining the common stages of wealth creation:

Foundation Stage: The foundation stage is the first stage of wealth building. It entails laying a sound financial foundation by emphasizing financial discipline and stability. Creating a budget, lowering debt, saving for an emergency, and developing solid financial habits are all important tasks to take during this time.

Income Growth Stage: The primary focus at this stage is on raising income and expanding earning potential. Career growth, learning new skills or education, pursuing higher-paying work possibilities, or starting a business are all examples of this. The purpose is to enhance the inflow of money to generate surplus.

Saving and Investing Stage: As income increases, the focus switches to saving and investing. Setting particular financial goals, such as saving for retirement, purchasing a home, or supporting children's education, is part of this stage. It is critical to establish a disciplined savings strategy and to investigate various investment possibilities, such as stocks, bonds, real estate, or retirement accounts.

Wealth Accumulation Stage: The emphasis throughout this stage is on accumulating wealth through constant saving and investing. Compounding is important because investments generate returns that are reinvested, resulting in faster wealth growth. It is critical to maintain a diverse investment portfolio, analyze investment performance regularly, and alter strategies as appropriate.

Stage of Business and Entrepreneurship: For people with an entrepreneurial attitude, this stage entails founding or expanding a business. Entrepreneurship can bring extra income streams, tax benefits, and the opportunity to create large wealth. Strategic planning, market analysis, risk management, and ongoing innovation are all required.

Stage of Asset Protection and Risk Management: As wealth rises, it becomes increasingly important to preserve assets and manage risks. This step entails estate planning, insurance coverage, trust creation, and risk management techniques implementation. Asset protection ensures that the money amassed is protected and can be passed down to future generations.

Legacy & Philanthropy Stage: This stage focuses on how to use collected money to make a long-term difference and leave a meaningful legacy. It entails charity donations, philanthropic activities, and estate planning to support causes or organizations that match personal ideals. It enables individuals to make a constructive contribution to society and have an impact on future generations.

It is crucial to note that these stages are not necessarily sequential, and people may shift between them as their circumstances change. Furthermore, the time it takes to proceed through each stage can differ based on factors such as income, market conditions, investment performance, and personal ambitions.

Chapter 3

Scaling and managing your income streams

Scaling and managing your income streams are essential for long-term success and financial stability. In this chapter, we will explore the key strategies and principles of scaling and managing your income streams effectively.

Evaluate Scalability Potential: Assess the scalability potential of each income stream. Consider factors such as market demand, available resources, scalability limitations, and your capacity to handle the increased workload. Identify income streams that have the potential for substantial growth and prioritize them for scaling.

Streamline Operations and Processes: To scale your income streams efficiently, it's crucial to streamline operations and processes. Automate repetitive tasks, optimize workflows, and leverage technology to increase efficiency. Streamlining operations allows you to handle higher volumes of work without sacrificing quality or consuming excessive time and resources.

Delegate and Outsource: As your income streams grow, consider delegating or outsourcing certain tasks to free up your time and focus on high-value activities. Identify areas where others can handle certain responsibilities, such as administrative tasks, customer support, or marketing. Delegation and outsourcing enable you to scale your income streams while maintaining productivity and quality.

Expand Your Reach: Explore opportunities to expand your reach and attract a wider audience for your income streams. Leverage social media platforms, implement effective marketing strategies, collaborate with influencers or complementary businesses, or target new geographic markets. Expanding your reach increases your customer base and revenue potential.

Set Financial Goals and Track Performance: Establish financial goals for each income stream and track their performance regularly. Monitor key metrics such as revenue, expenses, profit margins, and return on investment. By setting clear goals and tracking performance, you can identify areas for improvement and make informed decisions to optimize your income stream's financial outcomes.

Diversify Revenue Sources: Continuously seek opportunities to diversify your revenue sources within each income stream. Explore new products, services, or offerings that complement your existing offerings and cater to different customer segments. Diversification reduces the risk of relying heavily on a single product or service and opens up new avenues for growth.

Continuously Innovate and Improve: Stay proactive in innovating and improving your income streams. Monitor market trends, customer feedback, and industry developments to identify opportunities for innovation. Regularly update and refine your products, services, or offerings to stay ahead of the competition and meet evolving customer needs.

Nurture Customer Relationships: Building and maintaining strong customer relationships is crucial for the long-term success of your income streams. Focus on delivering exceptional customer experiences, providing value, and fostering loyalty. Implement customer retention strategies, such as personalized communication, loyalty programs, or exclusive offers, to cultivate repeat business and maximize customer lifetime value.

Plan for Contingencies and Risk Mitigation: Anticipate potential risks and plan for contingencies to safeguard your income streams. This includes having emergency funds, diversifying your client base, securing contracts or agreements, and maintaining a healthy financial buffer. Planning for contingencies helps you navigate unforeseen circumstances and minimizes the impact on your income streams.

Time Management and Work-Life Balance: Effective time management is essential when managing multiple income streams. Prioritize your tasks, set boundaries, and allocate time for each income stream accordingly. Strive for a healthy work-life balance to avoid burnout and maintain your productivity and focus. By implementing strategies to scale, streamline operations, diversify revenue sources, and manage your income streams proactively, you can unlock their full potential and achieve your income goals. Remember to regularly evaluate performance, adapt to market changes, and nurture customer relationships to ensure sustainable growth. In the next chapter, we will explore the importance of continuous learning and adaptation in the dynamic landscape of multiple income streams.

The *significance* of scaling and managing numerous income streams

Scaling and maintaining numerous income streams is critical for several reasons:

Increased Earning Potential: By diversifying your income, you can increase your earning potential. You can produce more revenue overall by developing and growing each income stream. Scaling allows you to enhance profitability by leveraging your existing resources, client base, and experience. It creates new prospects for financial success and growth.

Risk Reduction and Stability: These are provided by managing several income sources, which act as a buffer against economic uncertainties or interruptions in a specific industry or market. If one source of income experiences difficulties, others can continue to create revenue and give stability. Diversification across multiple sources helps to decrease risk, resulting in a more resilient and secure environment.

Diversification of Knowledge and Skills: Managing several streams of revenue exposes you to a variety of industries, business structures, and skill sets. You gain a wide set of abilities and expertise as you scale and manage each income stream. This broadens your knowledge, making you more adaptive and versatile in a variety of professional settings. Diversifying your abilities increases your marketability and opens up new chances.

Synergies: Managing various streams of income allows you to find and capitalize on synergies between your money-generating activities. Synergies can occur when one source of revenue complements or strengthens another. Skills and resources developed in one stream, for example, might be used in another, increasing efficiency and optimizing returns. You can achieve greater overall performance and efficiency by leveraging synergies.

Time and Materials Optimization: Scaling and maintaining various income streams necessitates efficient time management and resource allocation. It motivates you to prioritize activities, streamline procedures, and discover places for automation or delegation. Strategic optimization allows you to make the most use of your time and resources, ultimately increasing production and profitability.

Wealth Creation and Long-Term Financial Stability: Increasing the number of income streams is a means to increase wealth and long-term financial stability. You earn more money and raise your net worth as you scale each stream. The cumulative effect of scaling several streams can result in enormous wealth gain over time. This diversification of income sources also decreases reliance on a single source, laying the groundwork for long-term financial security.

Flexibility and Freedom: Managing various sources of income gives you more flexibility and freedom in determining your work-life balance. Scaling enables you to create a lifestyle that is in line with your goals and aspirations. You can build a more flexible schedule, choose projects or clients that interest you, and have the opportunity to pursue personal hobbies in addition to your revenue-generating activities by diversifying your income streams.

Entrepreneurial Opportunities: Managing and scaling various income streams frequently necessitates the creation of entrepreneurial companies. Scaling allows you to expand and grow your company operations, whether they are a side business, a consultancy, or an internet platform. As you grow, you will be able to enter new markets, attract more clients, and expand your influence and impact. Entrepreneurial prospects offer the possibility of financial benefits, personal development, and the satisfaction of creating something meaningful.

Professional Development and Mastery: Scaling numerous income streams necessitates ongoing learning, adaptation, and a relentless pursuit of greatness. You are motivated to increase your skills, knowledge, and efficiency as you manage and scale each stream. This dedication to professional development improves your expertise in numerous domains, presenting you as an expert and improving your market value.

Building a Legacy: Having many streams of income allows you to leave a lasting legacy. By establishing sustainable and profitable income streams, you can lay the groundwork for generational wealth and pass important assets down to future generations. It allows you to make a significant effect while also leaving a financial legacy.

Scaling and managing numerous income streams provide enhanced income potential, risk reduction, and diversification of talents and knowledge, utilizing synergies, time and resource optimization, wealth generation, flexibility, entrepreneurial chances, professional development, and the ability to leave a lasting legacy. You may build a resilient and profitable financial future through smart management and planned scaling.

Conclusion

Congratulations on finishing *"The Income Catalyst: Unleashing the Power of Multiple Streams of Income"*! Throughout this book, we have discussed the essential steps and strategies to generate, diversify, scale, and manage multiple streams of income. By taking advantage of the potential of multiple income streams, you have taken a big step towards financial independence and a more secure future. We began by evaluating your skills and passions, understanding market demand, and brainstorming income ideas. This process allowed you to identify income opportunities that fit your strengths and interests. Then, we looked into the important aspects of developing a strong personal brand, building credibility, and connecting with your target audience. With a strong foundation in place, we moved on to the core principles of scaling and managing your income streams. You learned how to evaluate scalability potential, streamline operations, delegate tasks, and expand your reach. We highlighted the importance of setting financial goals, tracking performance, diversifying revenue sources, and nurturing customer relationships.

Throughout this journey, you have gained insights into effective time management, the significance of continuous learning, and the value of adaptability in the ever-changing landscape of multiple income streams. You have discovered the power of resilience, resourcefulness, and strategic decision-making. It is important to remember that developing and managing multiple streams of income is not a quick process. It requires dedication, perseverance, and a willingness to embrace challenges and adapt to new opportunities. Your income portfolio will evolve, and you must remain agile and responsive to market trends and customer needs.

As you continue your journey, keep the following principles in mind: prioritize and focus on your income streams, continuously assess their performance, and look for ways to innovate and improve. Embrace the spirit of entrepreneurship, take calculated risks, and learn from both successes and failures. "The Income Catalyst" has given you the knowledge, tools, and mindset to create a diverse and resilient income portfolio. Remember that building multiple streams of income is not only about financial gain—it is about creating a life of freedom, flexibility, and fulfillment. Now, with the insights and strategies from this book, go forth and unleash the power of multiple streams of income. Embrace the possibilities, seize the opportunities, and pave your path to financial success and personal fulfillment. Your journey to financial independence starts now.